·the·
picnic

the
picnic

jane pettigrew

Publication in this form copyright © Jarrold Publishing 2006
Text copyright © Jane Pettigrew
The moral right of the author has been asserted
Series editor Jenni Davis
Designed by Mark Buckingham and Tim Noel-Johnson
Pictures researched by Jenni Davis

A CIP catalogue for this book is available from the British Library.

Published by:
Jarrold Publishing
Healey House, Dene Road, Andover, Hampshire, SP10 2AA
www.britguides.com

Set in Bembo
Printed in Singapore
ISBN-10: 1 84165 172 9
ISBN-13: 978 1 84165 172 9
1/06

Pitkin is an imprint of Jarrold Publishing, Norwich

contents

introduction

An early 20th-century poster of a perfect picnic and (above) a wartime picnic, illustrated on the cover of Homes and Gardens *in 1943.*

Murmur the word 'picnic' to yourself and allow your memory to recapture all those lost images. Floating to the surface come scenes of exquisite countryside and glorious views, cloudless skies and dazzling sunshine, children scampering after balls and kites, lazy adults lounging on cheerfully coloured rugs and blankets, nibbling at delicious food laid out on brightly decorated platters and dishes, idly chattering, browsing through newspapers, occasionally calling out to the young ones or joining their game of football or cricket or rounders. Glasses of wine nestle slightly askew among tufts of grass, a couple of broad-brimmed straw hats lie discarded near by, an open book sits face down where it was rejected in favour of a treasure hunt with the children or a game of hide-and-seek.

The simple pleasures of a picnic – good food, good wine and a shady spot beneath a tree. John Leech's cartoon in Punch, c.1850 (above), was captioned wryly: 'It would have been so provoking to have brought our umbrellas and then to have had a fine day!'

There is something that is intriguing, fascinating and immensely satisfying about arriving at a carefully chosen picnic spot – often in a somewhat straggly, disorganized fashion – and, from a motley collection of bags and baskets, rolled-up bundles and back packs, conjuring a delicious, colourful, creative feast that is always more exciting and tempting than any refreshment eaten indoors. Even when a picnic is a more practical meal to replenish energy burned up during an exhilarating hike or a day's ramble, the pleasures to be derived from eating in the open air are the same.

The world of work, responsibilities and daily chores can be temporarily forgotten while the peace of wide open skies, rolling countryside, hills and fields, woodland and wild flowers bring a unique sense of freedom. And even if the sky is not actually cloudless all day, and some essential part of the picnic equipment was forgotten, or one of the party fell and grazed a knee, those minor details are erased from the enduring memory of the day's events. It is the romance and fun, the sense of having escaped that remains with us and seduces us in the future to pack another picnic and head once again for the open country.

'The contemplation of so idyllic, so simple a delight holds a particular poignancy; yet of one thing you can be sure; whether or no the picnic is a true pleasure, the habit of it is so firmly engraved in human character that it will survive countless calamities and holocausts.'
Osbert Sitwell,
Picnics and Pavilions, 1944

defining the picnic

Although pilgrims, travellers and revellers have undoubtedly enjoyed meals in the open air since medieval times and beyond, the word 'picnic' did not make its entry into the English language until 1748,

A tottering tower of picnic sandwiches made with Hovis bread, from a 1950s advertisement. A jug of home-made lemonade (above) adds the finishing touch to a traditional picnic.

when it is thought to have derived from the French *pique-nique* – a term that marries the notion of *piquer* (meaning to nibble or peck at) with *nique* (a small trifle).

Original definitions describe this novel event as a 'fashionable social entertainment in which each person present contributed a share of the provisions'. In 1802, *The Times* reported: 'The subscribers to the entertainment have the bill of fare presented to them with a number against each dish. The lot which he draws obliges him to furnish the dish marked against it, which he either takes with him in his carriage or sends by servant.' In the same spirit, a picnic conversation was one in which each person involved in the proceedings contributed their fair share of wisdom and wit.

The term gradually acquired specific associations with alfresco eating and it is now understood – in the words of *The Oxford English Dictionary* – as 'a pleasure party including an excursion to some spot in the country where all partake of a repast out of doors'.

Come and get it!

It's only natural that healthy children should have hearty appetites for Hovis. They take kindly to Hovis and Hovis is kind to them. Helps them grow. Builds their strength the natural way.

With its extra wheatgerm Hovis is grand for children and a treat for all who know how bread should taste.

Hovis is the slice of life
so have some every day!

the first picnics

A detail from an early 15th-century tapestry depicting an outdoor banquet. The illustration above, from Through Merrie England *(1928), depicts a May-Day feast in the 17th century.*

One of the first outdoor meals to be recorded was chronicled by Reginald of Durham, who described the life of a group of monks from Lindisfarne; driven from their monastery by Viking invaders in the late 8th century, they travelled from place to place, carrying the remains of St Cuthbert's body. Wherever they stopped for rest, crowds would gather to pay tribute to the dead saint and offer sustenance to the monks. Gifts of bread and cheese were welcome but soon devoured, and all that was left at one point was the salted head of a horse. Reginald reported how the hungry band had reached 'the vast confines of the desolate country of the Picts and the brethren, having spread a tablecloth over their knees, sat down on the ground to a lowly table in the lap of the earth' to draw what nourishment they could from the meagre provisions.

Through medieval times, important days in the annual calendar were celebrated with feasts and festivities, often in the open air. Froissart, a French diarist, wrote of his life in England in his *Espinette Amoureuse* and told how, on the first of May, he and his fellow revellers 'came to a place made for our pleasant repose; here let us break our fast! Then with one accord we brought out the meats, pasties, hams, wines and bakemeats, and venison packed in heather. Then was my lady ruler of the feast.'

'I walked the length of the Elmes and with great pleasure saw some gallant ladies and people come with their bottles and baskets, and chairs, and form, to sup under the trees by the waterside, which was mighty pleasant.'
Samuel Pepys at Barne Elmes

georgian and regency picnics

Picnics have been a favourite subject for works of art for many centuries. Dartmouth Cove *was painted by Joseph Mallord Turner (1775–1851), while* A Picnic: Two Ladies and a Gentleman *(above) is the work of Hubert Gravelot (1699–1773).*

Although the word 'picnic' was not current in the English language when George I ascended the throne in 1714, outdoor feasts in the gardens and parks of aristocratic mansions and on ornate barges on the river were a popular entertainment. The grounds of country houses were elaborately laid out with lakes, follies, gazebos, grottoes and pavilions, the summer venue for grand excursions and open-air feasts.

The Prince of Wales (later George IV) continued the fashion for extravagant outdoor entertaining. Staying at the Royal Pavilion in Brighton in 1789, he celebrated his birthday with 'mirth and festivity heretofore unknown in this country … The morning was ushered in with ringing of bells, etc, etc. Between 11 and 12 o'clock, His Royal Highness, accompanied by his Royal brothers, Mrs Fitzherbert, Mr Fox, and a great number of the Nobility, etc,

repaired to a plain adjacent to the town … An ox was roasted whole near the spot, and liquor was set in hogsheads in the open field for the population, who were exceedingly numerous.'

In the early 19th century, the Prince and Mrs Fitzherbert (his mistress) founded the Picnic Club and the group's activities included theatrical presentations, accompanied by a picnic supper. Following the royal example, people all over Britain enjoyed forays into the countryside for a sociable day in the fresh air and cold collations of pigeon pies, ham and roast beef.

Jane Austen's fictitious benefactor Sir John Middleton, who offered Barton Cottage to the Dashwoods in *Sense and Sensibility,* 'was a blessing to all the juvenile part of the neighbourhood, for in the summer he was for ever forming parties to eat cold ham and chicken out of doors …'.

london's pleasure gardens

This 1808 aquatint of Vauxhall Gardens appeared in Rudolph Ackermann's Microcosm of London. *Above, an 18th-century aquatint illustrates the Chinese House and Rotunda in Ranalagh Gardens.*

The pleasure gardens of 18th-century London offered their visitors tea with bread and butter as a standard part of the entertainment, but regular *fêtes champêtres* on a European scale added to the attraction of the larger, more famous gardens. Vauxhall, on the south side of the river, was popular for its lanterns and lamps, torches and flares, music by Mozart and Haydn, firework displays, expansive tableaux, masked balls and brightly painted supper boxes where elaborate feasts might be enjoyed in the open air.

Lighter, alfresco refreshments were the norm in all the gardens around the capital. At Finch's Grotto Garden in Southwark, 'the gardens were open on Sunday when sixpence was charged, though a visitor was entitled for his money to tea, half a pint of wine, cakes, jelly or cyder.' Pancras Wells in north London was frequented in the 1760s and 70s 'as a genteel and rural tea garden', with its hot loaves, syllabubs and milk from the cow, and the Adam and Eve in Tottenham served tea in shady arbours. Dinners could also be obtained, along with neat wines, curious punch, Dorchester, Ringwood and Marlborough beers.

Sadler's Wells in Islington had a monopoly on the sales of cakes, milks, custards, stewed prunes and bottled ale, while the Rotunda at Ranalagh in Chelsea, according to a certain Miss Lydia Melford, 'was crowded with the great, the rich, the gay, the happy, and the fair. While these exulting sons and daughters of felicity tread this round of pleasure, or regale in different parties, and separate lodges, with fine tea and other delicious refreshments, their ears are entertained with the most ravishing delights of music, both instrumental and vocal.'

the sandwich and its inventor

The evolution of the sandwich – this modern version is a far cry from Lord Sandwich's invention. In the painting above, c.1771 by John Hamilton Mortimer, Lord Sandwich poses with Captain Cook, founder of the Sandwich Islands.

Although picnics today usually include more creative finger food than just slices of meat, cheese or eggs laid between two slices of bread, the sandwich is still an extremely useful (and potentially delicious) part of any packed meal. It is thought that the conquering Romans were responsible for teaching the Britons how to eat something called *offula* – apparently rather like a modern sandwich – and it is likely that, through the following centuries, hungry mortals found that bread offered the perfect wrap for tasty, nourishing fillings. But the snack food did not gain its name and place in British history until 1762 when John Montague, Fourth Earl of Sandwich, called for some roast beef between two layers of bread to enable him to satisfy his hunger (and avoid greasy fingers) while he indulged in his favourite pastime – gambling. His name quickly became associated with this most convenient manner of eating and others also started ordering their own choice of sandwich. Although best known for his layered lunch, the Earl was actually employed as First Lord of the Admiralty and financed the expedition of Captain Cook, who named the Sandwich Islands after him.

Variations of the sandwich are eaten worldwide. In Greece, pockets of pitta bread are stuffed with feta cheese, sliced red onions, olives and homous or taramasalata. In the south of France, Pan Bagnat is made from bread soaked in olive oil and filled with salad. In Sweden, the Låndganger is an open sandwich of bread, herrings, pâté, cold roast beef, cheese and mayonnaise that keeps farm workers going through the afternoon. And the now ubiquitous burger is, of course, the American twist on the Earl's gambling picnic.

victorian picnics

Victorian families picnic on London's Hampstead Heath, still a much-loved venue today. Above, a postcard depicting Queen Victoria's Prime Minister William Ewart Gladstone picnicking with his wife and their friends.

For the Victorians, the term 'picknickery and nicknackery' signified something frivolous, inconsequential and even a little risqué – but the picnic itself represented escape. For the wealthy, it meant escape from the rigours of formal dining and the stiff, unrelenting rules of etiquette; for the poor, it promised escape from the grubby, overcrowded, unhealthy streets of the large industrial towns. With the coming of the railways and with a new enthusiasm for cycling, walking and exploring, town dwellers spilled out into the cleaner, greener parts of Britain to fill their lungs with fresh air and enjoy the visual delights of the countryside. Queen Victoria herself developed a passion for the freedom of the great outdoors, away from the stuffiness and rigidity of life in the royal palaces.

Members of various organizations – church groups, archaeological societies, architectural associations, walking and cycling clubs – set off to discover unknown places, with sketchbooks and diaries to record their adventures in heathland and forest, hills and dales, and the butterflies, birds and flowers they saw. Diarist Edward Fitzgerald described a typical picnic in Ireland in 1843: 'We have at last delightful weather and we enjoy it. Yesterday we went to Pool-a Phooka, the Leap of the Goblin Horse. What is that, do you suppose? Why, a cleft in the mountains, down through which the river Liffey comes leaping and racing. Cold veal pies, champagne, etc. make up the enchantment. We dabbled in the water, splashed each other, forded the river, climbed the rocks, laughed, sang, eat, drink, and were toasted, and returned home, the sun sinking fast.'

a picnic with mrs beeton

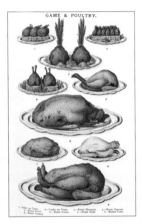

The front cover of an 1890 edition of Mrs Beeton's classic book, Every Day Cookery and Housekeeping. The plate from the 1907 edition (above) shows a selection of roast game and poultry – perfect food for a picnic.

Isabella Beeton, despite her remarkable youth (she died at the age of 27), was an accomplished and practical cook and housekeeper who offered a good deal of extremely sensible advice to readers on all aspects of family life, including how to cater for a picnic.

Mrs Beeton's suggested 'Bill of Fare for Forty Persons' listed the following items of food and drink:

A joint of cold roast beef, a joint of cold boiled beef, 2 ribs of lamb, 2 shoulders of lamb, 4 roast fowls, 2 roast ducks, 1 ham, 1 tongue, 2 veal-and-ham pies, 2 pigeon pies, 6 medium sized lobsters, 1 piece of collared calf's head, 18 lettuces, 6 baskets of salad, 6 cucumbers.

Stewed fruit all sweetened and put into glass bottles well corked; 3 or 4 dozen plain pastry biscuits to eat with the stewed fruit. 2 dozen fruit turnovers, 4 dozen cheesecakes, 2 cold cabinet puddings in moulds, 2 blancmanges in moulds, a few jam puffs, 1 large cold plum-pudding (this must be good), a few baskets of fruit, 3 dozen plain biscuits, a piece of cheese, 6lbs of butter (this, of course, includes the butter for tea), 4 quartern loaves of household bread, 3 dozen rolls, 6 loaves of tin bread (for tea), 2 plain plum cakes, 2 pound cakes, 2 sponge cakes, a tin of mixed biscuits, ½lb of tea. Coffee is not suitable for a picnic, being difficult to make.

Beverages – 3 dozen quart bottles of ale, packed in hampers; ginger-beer, soda-water, and lemonade, of each 2 dozen bottles; 6 bottles of sherry, 6 bottles of claret, champagne à discrétion, and any other light wine that may be preferred, and 2 bottles of brandy. Water can usually be obtained so it is useless to take it.

MRS·BEETON'S
EVERY DAY
COOKERY
AND
·HOUSE·KEEPING·BOOK·

Entirely
New Edition
Revised
and
Greatly Enlarged

NEW·COLOURED·PLATES
and full page & other Engravings

queen victoria's picnics

A sepia photograph of Queen Victoria and her family taken on the terrace at Osborne House in 1857. Above, Victoria and Albert picnic at Carn Lochan, near Balmoral, in October 1861, just a few weeks before the prince's untimely death.

Queen Victoria loved spending time in the fresh air at Osborne House on the Isle of Wight: 'The whole Royal family, children, Queen and all, seem to be out the whole day long ... the children dine and tea in the garden, and run about to their heart's content ....' The Queen herself described how 'we breakfasted out of doors and were much amused in watching the children running about and climbing.'

Victoria seemed to enjoy the bracing temperatures of the British climate and was always enthusiastic about jaunts to the countryside, especially in Scotland where she and Albert had several happy holidays. In 1863, Victoria's Prime Minister Disraeli wrote from Balmoral after a day's outing with the Queen, 'We seldom come in till nine and yesterday at ten, having taken our tea with some meat out of doors.' And in 1868, Disraeli told his wife in a letter,

'Yesterday we went on one of those expeditions you read of in the Queen's book, two carriages posting and changing horses. We went to the castle of Braemar ... Then we drove to the Linn of Lee – a fall of the Dee river. On the bank we lunched. One might take many hints for country luncheons from this day ....'

In October 1866, the Queen wrote in 'More Leaves from the Journal of our Life in the Highlands': 'The evening was quite splendid, the sky yellow and pink and the distant hills coming out soft and blue ... at a place called Loch-na-Braig – we stopped, and while Grant ran back to get from a small house some hot water in the kettle, we three, with Brown's help, scrambled over a low stone wall by the roadside, and lit a fire and prepared our tea. The kettle soon returned, and the hot tea was very welcome and refreshing.'

edwardian seaside picnics

A charming watercolour, painted by Helen Bradley in 1972, depicting an Edwardian seaside scene. Arthur Rackham's painting (above) shows children modestly attired in late-Edwardian bathing dress.

At the turn of the 19th century, the dark, heavy styles of Victorian Britain gave way to the Edwardian taste for brighter, softer fashions and a more frivolous and light-hearted way of life. And so, when it came to high days and holidays, the seaside promenades were thronged with gentlemen in bowler hats and bow ties accompanied by elegant ladies clad in white gowns and large, wide-brimmed hats and absent-mindedly twirling their parasols as they strolled in the sea breeze. Children scampered to and fro, dressed neatly in mini sailor-suits, but once they reached the sandy beach, off came the spotless outfits and on went the button-through hand-knitted swimsuits that stretched uncontrollably after a dip in the sea. And, after building a sandcastle, riding on a donkey, paddling in rock pools in search of crabs and shrimps, nothing could be more welcome than a picnic on the beach. Out of Mother's basket appeared ham sandwiches, egg sandwiches, roast beef sandwiches, bottles of home-made lemonade and home-made cakes. The sandwiches lived up to their name as the wind whipped gritty sand onto sticky fingers and sticky lips, and into all the food – but somehow sand and sandwiches seemed perfect partners.

'And, with boatmen so beguiling,
    sev'ral parties go out sailing!
Sitting all together smiling,
    handing sandwiches about,
To the sound of concertina –
    till they're gradually greener
And they wish the ham was leaner,
    as they sip their bottled stout.'
Anon, *The Joys of The Seaside*, 1888

26

picnics with purpose

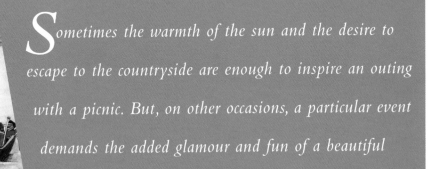

A royal hunt picnic, from the poet Turberville's 16th-century book The Noble Art of Venerie. *Peter Miller's amusing 1992 painting (above) shows a rather less noble group heading across the River Thames at the Henley Regatta.*

meal served with flourish and style to enhance that concert, opera, theatrical performance or sporting event. Such picnics need careful planning so that the menu and style suit the season, the traditions and the setting of the occasion. One must consider how the table is to be decorated, how the food is to be transported, presented and garnished, how beverages may be chilled and elegantly served, and how the guests are to be conveyed to the venue. Every detail must be carefully planned well in advance.

As Lady Colin Campbell explained in *The Etiquette of Good Society*, 1895: 'In reality an excursion of this kind entails much labour and thought on the getters-up! ... The first thing to plan ... must be how to convey your guests there. If possible, they should go in different ways ... The provisions should have a separate vehicle allotted to them, and not be scattered about ..., a basket stowed away in one corner, a hamper thrust under another seat, and so forth. No, a light cart is the best kind of conveyance for the delicacies.'

hunting picnics

The idea of an organized outdoor feast for huntsmen dates from the hunting festivities of medieval Europe. A formal open-air meal became an established ritual that took place before the huntsmen set off in pursuit of deer. Strict rules of etiquette about how to conduct such an event were the same throughout Europe – the 15th-century French publication *The Master of the Game* explained that 'the place where the gathering shall be made shall be in a fair mead, well green, where fair trees grow all about, the one far from the other, or beside some running brook … And all the officers that come from home shall bring thither all they need – and should lay the tables and board cloths all about upon the green grass and set diverse meats upon a great platter. And some should eat sitting, and some standing, and some leaning upon their elbows, some should drink, some joke, some play, in short, do all manner of disport and gladness.'

One wealthy Prince Bishop, who ruled over the lands between the River Tees and the River Tweed, had a great hall built each summer for the hunting season. It measured 60 feet long and 16 feet wide and comprised a buttery, chamber, kitchen, larder and chapel – all for the provision of food and comfort for the members of the hunting party.

'The Gathering before the Stag Hunt', an illustration in a medieval illuminated manuscript. A 1935 advertisement for Thermos (right) offers the comfort of hot food when your horse has left you stranded in a ditch!

shooting picnics

Victorian shooting parties at luncheon, depicted in The First of October, 1881 *by Edith Hayller and (above) in an illustration from the 28 October 1871 edition of* The Graphic.

Lady Harriet St Clair instructed in 1862, in *Dainty Dishes,* that gentlemen usually prefer eating their hunting picnic 'about the middle of the day, in the open air, with their fingers, in order that they may lose no time. So it is not generally necessary to send knives and forks or tablecloths; but you must take care, in order not to make them angry, that the luncheon is there at the right time and place.'

Up to the mid 19th century, shooting parties would carry a modest picnic with them and stop at an appropriate point in the proceedings to satisfy their hunger. Bread and cheese, cold meats, ale and cider were all that was needed. But during the Victorian era, shooting became a sport for gentlemen and so the refreshments took on a very much grander role. Marquees were erected and trestle tables set up, covered with crisp white linen cloths and arranged elegantly with gleaming silver cutlery, bone china and crystal glasses (all of which was carried out from the house by the servants). Whereas the hunting picnic of earlier years had simply been a quick pause for refreshment, it now expanded to consist of four or five courses and lasted for as long as two hours. The gamekeepers, beaters, gun loaders, ladies and gentlemen were fed hot stews, casseroles, meat puddings and pies, baked ham, jacket potatoes, steamed puddings, fruit pies, custards, cakes and cheeses, beers, ales, cider, brandy and gin. The hot dishes were carried out from the house wrapped in thick sacking or hidden inside hay boxes to keep them warm.

Today's shooting parties often eat indoors, especially if the weather is cold, but the quantity of hot foods and alcoholic drinks served can still match that consumed by the Victorians.

fishing picnics

A relaxed fishing picnic depicted in George Morland's The Angler's Repast. *In Winchester Cathedral, a stained-glass window (above) shows Izaak Walton, author of* The Compleat Angler, *sharing a fishing picnic in Dovedale with his friend Charles Cotton.*

Fishing is generally a rather solitary, calm and reflective activity (indeed this fact, and not the catching of fish, is perhaps a large part of the appeal), and it is important to be prepared with a good sustaining picnic meal that will add to the pleasure of the time spent at the waterside, whether it be a river bank or the seashore.

Nothing fancy is required but it should be tasty, satisfying fare that the fisherman really looks forward to unwrapping – chunky fresh bread with mature cheddar and tomato relish, juicy roast beef with wholegrain mustard and slices of firm tomato, or perhaps a meat pasty that bursts with flavour at the first bite. And for liquid refreshment, a bottle or two of beer or a wonderfully dry cider, kept cool inside a net bag suspended in the running water until thirst demands to be satisfied.

In 1653, Izaak Walton, who famously wrote 'I have laid aside business and gone fishing', included the following advice in his book *The Compleat Angler:*

'My honest scholar, it is now past five o'clock, we will fish till nine, and then go to breakfast. Go to yon sycamore-tree and hide your bottle of drink under the hollow root of it; for about that time, and in that place, we will make a brave breakfast with a piece of powdered beef, and a radish or two that I have in my fish-bag; we shall, I warrant you, make a good honest, wholesome, hungry breakfast ....'

harvest picnics

Some things stay the same over centuries: Haymakers at Dinner, a watercolour painted by Thomas Unwins (1782–1857), and (above) a page from Simon Bening's Book of Hours c.1540, with a harvest picnic in the foreground.

Ever since fields were planted with crops that fed the population and made money for the farmer, harvest time has demanded the toil of farm labourers and bands of itinerant workers who need sustenance throughout the day. Over the centuries, workers' hunger has been satisfied with generous hunks of bread and cheese, pies and pasties, salt herrings on fish days, and flagons of locally brewed ale and cider. Indeed, the now famous 'ploughman's lunch' that is offered in pubs and inns all over Britain originates from the idea that harvesters and farm workers always lunched off bread, cheese and pickles. The story goes that a gentleman farmer by the name of Sir Richard Trehane went into a pub in Surrey in 1954 and demanded a lunch of crusty bread and cheese 'fit for a ploughman', and since that day pubs have included the platter on their lunch-time menus.

In the days before thermos flasks and ice boxes were invented, the harvesters' food and drink, including hot tea, were carried out to the fields at midday by the women of the farm. Scythes and pitchforks were set aside and the hot and weary workers settled down in the shade of a haystack or under a nearby tree to tuck into their picnic. Then it was back to work among the ripe corn and fields of freshly mown hay.

'It was one o'clock and the haymakers left off their work and sat down in a row by the brook-side to eat their dinner … Lucy and Emily spread a clean napkin on the grass on which they placed the knives and forks and plates, with the loaf and meat, and the fruit pie, and a bottle of beer for their papa.'
Mrs Sherwood, *The Fairchild Family* (written between 1818 and 1847)

a day at the races

A watercolour depicting Edwardian racing enthusiasts at Royal Ascot, painted by John Strickland Goodall (1909–96). Above, another prestigious event is recorded by George Tattersall in The Goodwood Cup, 1845.

For centuries, racecourses have attracted all types of people who go there for a variety of reasons – simply to watch the horses, or to have a flutter and perhaps win a little (or sometimes a lot of) extra cash, perhaps to show off a new hat on 'Ladies' Day', enjoy the air, or take the children to one of the family days with funfairs, big wheels, animal farms, bouncy castles, face-painting, competitions and games.

And a well-planned picnic is always part of the entertainment. At Ascot, Number 1 Car Park is the best place for an elegant picnic and, as at other events during the London 'Season', the food is fancy, the champagne expensive and the strawberries absolutely bathed in cream; at Kempton Park, families are welcome to take picnics into the centre of the course; at Aintree, there is space in the Steeplechase Enclosure where picnics may be consumed before the Grand National and other events; at Newcastle, picnics are allowed in the Grandstand and Paddock Enclosure where tables and chairs are provided; and at the Epsom Derby, racegoers picnic or set up their barbecues on The Hill looking down over the course.

If the weather is kind, a day at the races can be great fun for everyone. And if you manage to back the right horse, even better!

'Things not to be forgotten …
A stick of horseradish, a bottle of
mint sauce well corked, a bottle of
salad dressing, a bottle of vinegar,
made mustard, pepper, salt, good oil,
and pounded sugar. If it can be
managed, take a little ice ….'
Mrs Isabella Beeton,
Book of Household Management, 1861

a picnic at henley

Under the Trees,
Henley Royal Regatta,
1987, *a depiction of this
London 'Season' event by
Sherree Valentine-Daines.
A generous supply of
Pimm's (above) is an
essential ingredient of a
successful Henley picnic.*

Picnics at Henley Regatta, the famous celebration of rowing and sculling held annually in June, are often much more about the liquid refreshment than prettily presented food.

For regular Henley revellers, the day by the River Thames might start with a Buck's Fizz breakfast party at home before wending an already slightly tipsy way to the appointed viewing spot in the Steward's Enclosure, in one of the grandstands neatly ranged along the waterside, or – perhaps best of all – in an open boat moored along the river bank. Although the sporting events start in the morning, spectators often don't arrive until midday – just in time to take a pre-lunch glass of champagne or a pint of minty Pimm's. The total number of bottles of celebratory drinks amounts each year to rather more than 50,000 bottles of Pimm's and some 6,000 bottles of champagne.

Those revellers who take their own picnic feast set up tables and dress them perfectly with linen tablecloths and vases of flowers, silver cutlery and crystal wine glasses. From hampers and baskets appear whole dressed salmon, salmon en croûte, beef Wellington, seafood salads and an impressive array of other pukka picnic treats. With every inch of grass occupied, car boots often serve as a perching place for picnickers while others relax in fold-up chairs. For those who prefer to take pot luck, there are oyster bars and beer tents, hamburgers and pints of prawns, and of course, afternoon tea in the corporate enclosures.

Henley is another of those eccentric events that go to make up the London 'Season'. It has its own quirky rules and regulations, involves a good deal of drinking, and provides enormous fun for everyone there.

a picnic at the opera

Images of the famous lake at Glyndebourne, painted in tempera in 1997 by Luke Ariel. The costumes above were designed for the Glyndebourne performance in 1948 of Mozart's comic opera Così fan Tutte.

In 1934, George and Audrey Christie hosted the first Glyndebourne Festival at their home in Sussex, and the Glyndebourne Festival Opera still performs there each summer from May until August. The Christies' son George and his wife Patricia have continued and expanded the festival, which today attracts visitors from all over the world. The joy of a visit to Glyndebourne has always been the perfect blend of an English stately home, an exquisite, quintessentially English garden, the performance of sublime music and the opportunity to dine alfresco in a truly elegant and inspiring setting.

Despite the walk from the car park to the garden where picnics are enjoyed in the interval, opera-loving picnickers expend a great deal of effort and care to ensure that their meals suit the occasion in style and content. Bottles of champagne nestle in buckets of ice, colourfully creative salads accompany poached salmon and succulent lobster, fat scarlet strawberries cluster beneath snowy white peaks of whipped cream, and summer puddings fairly burst with juicy red fruits.

For those who have neither the time nor the inclination to create such a feast for themselves, Glyndebourne caterers offer a variety of ready-made picnics that include such treats as asparagus with smoked salmon or potted crab, fillet of beef, tuna niçoise, or confit of salmon, followed by chocolate torte or panforte and a platter of carefully selected cheeses. Tables and chairs are available for hire, as are the services of a porter who will carry and arrange all the essential items and help make the occasion entirely trouble-free – leaving music-lovers at ease to satisfy both their appetites and their passion for the opera.

a hiking picnic

A poster recommending East Coast Joys, a visit to the drier side of Britain for the comfort of the hiker. A picnic rucksack (above) is perfect for hikers who like luxury with their lunch.

If a picnic lunch comes in the middle of a day of cross-country rambling or energetic scrambling up and down steep hillsides and along rough country footpaths, the midday refreshment needs to be packed into one of today's practical, weatherproof backpacks. These clever carriers include a number of ingenious little compartments and pockets that are designed for maps and compasses, gadgets and rain hats as well as food boxes and thermos flasks. Some even have separate sections for chilled wine bottles, and flaps that unzip and fold down to reveal the necessary tablewares, and also act as a neat little serving area.

Choose lightweight plastic bottles and boxes and, instead of traditional knives and forks, save space with travelling cutlery sets or fold-away penknives that hide knife, fork and spoon, bottle opener and corkscrew.

By manoeuvring small insulated bags, boxes, bottles and ice packs into every available inch of space, hikers can suit their menu to the weather and tuck into piping hot soup or creamy hot chocolate on a bitterly cold winter's day, or sip chilled white wine with smoked salmon or prawn sandwiches in midsummer – a triumphant reward for a morning's hearty exercise! Unclip your roll-up picnic blanket from a hook on your belt, spread out in a comfortable spot where the view inspires and tuck in.

'1792 June 13th
We crept through a boggy wood into a field and there, opening our budget … we eat and drank voraciously.'
Lord Torrington,
The Torrington Diaries

N.º 1 WALKING TOURS

EAST COAST JOYS
travel by L·N·E·R
TO THE DRIER SIDE OF BRITAIN

setting the scene

*P*icnics linger more clearly in the memory when the menu has been planned and the food presented with as much care as is taken for a dinner party at home. Whether it is to be laid out on the ground or served on a table top, the cloth should

A little imagination goes a long way to setting an attractive picnic scene – a throw suspended on poles, a pretty tablecloth, the odd cushion tossed carelessly, and (above) a basket of flowers to complete the effect.

be brightly coloured; if the ground on which the cloth is to be spread is damp, lay a waterproof groundsheet or large plastic bin liners underneath. Choose cloth, napkins, crockery and cutlery that match or complement each other and, once the cloth has been settled in a suitable spot, lay places for each picnicker and arrange the platters and dishes of food in the middle. Strew leaves and flowers on the cloth or, if using a picnic table, add a vase of grasses and decorative twigs and leaves (or flowers brought from home).

Once everything has been unpacked, tidy away the clutter, leaving perhaps just the hamper near by – its rustic style and quintessential picnic quality adds to the effectiveness of the scene.

'Twenty minutes passed during which the gentlemen stood around the fire staring at the pot, while the ladies got flowery wreaths and green and wild roses to adorn the dishes and tablecloth spread under an oak tree and covered with provisions.'
Francis Kilvert's Diary, June 1870

picnic furniture

A folding table and chairs are perfect for taking on a picnic as they can be set up in seconds – an old set with a 'lived-in' look adds character to the setting. A humane wasp trap (above) is a must to divert the attentions of those uninvited guests.

Although for some picnickers, chairs and tables are unnecessary to the enjoyment of their outing, others prefer a certain amount of comfort and so, whenever possible, include fold-away tables and chairs in the list of essentials. And there are plenty to choose from – lightweight fold-up tables with telescopic legs that adjust to cope with uneven ground; neat circular wooden tables with slatted tops and hinged legs; metal and plastic trestles with sturdy legs and easy-clean surfaces. Seating also comes in a wide range of options – waterproof air-filled cushions that add comfort at ground level; fabric directors' chairs that sometimes have a fold-out table; metal and plastic diners with collapsible legs; adjustable reclining deck chairs and retro-classic ring chairs that fold flat, comfortable loungers with sunshades for babies and older children; and you can even snooze after an indulgent picnic lunch in a fold-away rocking chair or rocking lounger.

To hold tablecloths in place, pack coloured or transparent café clips that snap onto the edges of most table tops. And remember to pack mosquito and bug repellents and wasp traps that attract the insects away from you and your meal.

'It is the novelty which is the great charm, for the same set of people whom you now see making merry over the salt and the sugar and who declare it to be the summit of human felicity to sit in an uncomfortable position upon something never intended to be a seat, – these same people would grumble loudly did such things occur daily.'
Lady Colin Campbell,
The Etiquette of Good Society, 1895

picnic tablewares

Pink is glorious for a colour coordinated picnic as it's the perfect partner for the fresh, natural green of the countryside. A mesh food cover (above) is very useful for keeping bugs at bay.

To create a really pleasing picnic, colour-coordinate your tablewares with tablecloths and rugs. Most picnic bags and hampers come ready packed with matching sets of plates, cups and bowls, but if you need to start from scratch, tough unbreakable picnic wares made from plastic, acrylic, poly-carbon and melamine are readily available in a rainbow range of colours. Add clear or brightly coloured water jugs, ice buckets, wine glasses, tumblers, hi-ball glasses, dessert bowls and serving dishes, salad bowls with matching servers, dinner plates, side plates and mugs. To save on space, especially on a walking tour or ramble, take telescopic plastic drinking glasses. To enjoy your drinks at the required temperature, serve them in double-walled glasses, and for ease of tea- and coffee-brewing and drinking, use insulated mugs with infuser baskets and sipper lids.

Plastic cutlery is lighter to carry than stainless steel and can add more colour to the table when knives, forks and spoons coordinate with or complement the colours of plates and dishes. Also useful when flies and wasps threaten to invade your food, see-through mesh umbrellas keep out all those unwanted creatures but allow picnickers to enjoy the visual effect of a carefully laid-out sumptuous feast.

'Hence rustic dinners on the cool
*   green ground,*
Or in the woods, or by a river's side
Or shady fountains, while among
*   the leaves*
Soft airs were stirring, and the
*   midday sun*
Unfelt shone brightly round us in
*   our joy.'*
William Wordsworth, *The Prelude*

the picnic hamper

A stack of Fortnum & Mason's famous picnic hampers. Picnics have come a very long way since Dick Whittington set out with his kerchief on a stick, depicted above in Peeps into the Past, *published c.1900.*

Dick Whittington (*c.*1358–1423), the legendary Mayor of London, is said to have carried his meagre victuals in a kerchief knotted around the end of a stick and carried over his shoulder, but fortunately outdoor dining has become a little more sophisticated since those days. As trips into the countryside became more popular, the enterprising victuallers Fortnum & Mason started selling luxury picnic hampers filled with indulgent treats. Since 1788, the company's very successful hampers have included such delicacies as 'boned portions of poultry and game, eggs in brandy-soaked cake with whipped cream'. And in the early days of rail travel, rail companies provided hampers at a cost of only three shillings, which bought chicken and ham salad, bread, butter and cheese, a bottle of wine, crockery and cutlery – all packed into a sturdy, returnable wicker basket.

Today, more elaborate and creative meals can be conjured out of hampers and baskets that hold all the necessary equipment and still have room for provisions. Picnickers can choose from a wide variety of containers (some in natural wicker, others in pale creams or whites or even very bold black), all of which open to reveal crockery, cutlery, glasses, cups and saucers in a range of pretty summery colours, as well as a selection of lidded boxes and bottles. The best hamper is one that has a level bottom, is not too heavy, has a very secure handle and can be carried flat if necessary – so has a handle on each side as well as or instead of only on the front or top.

'… strawberries (by the hamperful) were bought from Betty, the fruit girl.' Horace Walpole on picnicking at Vauxhall Pleasure Gardens

packing the perfect picnic

This 1920s poster shows the new and chic way to travel to a picnic. If you don't have a vintage car like this at your disposal, retro-style thermos flasks (above) add a rather more accessible touch of nostalgia.

Nothing spoils a picnic more than opening bags and baskets and finding that things have spilled and broken. The efficient Isabella Beeton knew how important were the preparations for a successful outing. In *Every Day Cookery* she wrote, 'Little mistakes will invariably occur at all picnics … Things will be forgotten; some viands possibly spoilt by bad packing, and such like small troubles ….'

The number of hampers, baskets, bags and bundles taken on a picnic must depend on whether the food and drink are to be carried as refreshment on a walking excursion or delivered by car, bus, train or other means of transport. The latter will involve the question of how close the chosen vehicle can convey the picnickers and picnic to the appointed location.

When all the essential food and drink have been gathered together, use every inch of space inside the chosen carrying containers to pack everything safely and securely. Pack small items such as salt and pepper pots and little jars of mustard, salad dressing, etc. inside cups and glasses, padded with paper towel. Roll napkins around cutlery to prevent them from rattling. Fill any spaces with paper towels, plastic bags and tea towels. Place anything that may be inclined to spill or leak inside air-tight lidded boxes and – just to be quite sure – inside a layer of cling film or a plastic bag.

Arrange heavier, more solid items at the bottom of bags, leaving space on top for squashables and breakables such as fruit, platters of cheese and fragile desserts. And it is a good idea to pack a few nibbles on the very top just in case some members of the party demand refreshment before the picnic is actually set up.

pepper salad

This can be made up and carried in a plastic container or used to fill a crisp pastry base.

5 red peppers
5 yellow peppers
1 red chilli
1 shallot
2 cloves of garlic
3 tbsp extra virgin olive oil
salt and pepper
a handful of fresh basil
2 tbsp balsamic vinegar

Either grill or toast over a gas flame the red and yellow peppers until they are charred black. Put in a plastic bag to steam; when cool, peel the blackened skin off and clean under running water. Slice the peppers thinly into a bowl. De-seed and finely chop the chilli, finely chop the shallot, cut the garlic into fine slithers and add them all to the peppers with the olive oil. Season with salt and pepper and a handful of torn basil leaves. Reduce the balsamic vinegar in a small non-reactive saucepan over a high heat until it becomes syrup-like. Drizzle over the salad.

Fabulous picnic food – a roasted pepper salad served in a crisp pastry case, and (above) a filling, delicious and easy-to-carry Spanish tortilla.

spanish tortilla

2 large onions
500g (1lb 2oz) new potatoes
1 red chilli
1 head of garlic
12 eggs
salt and pepper
a handful each of thyme, parsley, tarragon
corn oil for cooking

Chop the onions finely and the potatoes into even chunks about 2cm (1in) square (do not peel). De-seed and chop the chilli. Peel the garlic cloves. Put the onions, potatoes, chilli and garlic into a large frying pan and cover with oil (don't worry – this is all drained off). Cook over a medium heat until they are

all just cooked through (do not brown). Drain off the oil. Wipe the frying pan. Beat the eggs and season generously with salt and pepper. Add the chopped herbs. Over a gentle heat, pour half the eggs into the pan, arrange the potatoes and onions on the top and cover with the remaining egg. Cook gently until you see that it has cooked half the thickness of the tortilla. Either put under a grill to cook the top or finish off in the oven. Cooking time is about an hour, but it is well worth the wait.

marinated fish salad

This marinated fish salad 'cooks' itself in its dressing, and is wonderful served with a lavishly decorated slab of corn bread (above).

1kg (2lb 2oz) white fish (cod, haddock, monkfish)
1 shallot, finely chopped
2 cloves of garlic, finely chopped
zest and juice of 2 large juicy lemons
100ml (4fl oz) water
2 tspn sea salt
freshly ground black pepper to taste
1 tspn sugar
1 red chilli, finely chopped
3 handfuls of chopped fresh mixed herbs
(parsley, basil, fennel)

Slice the fish into 1cm ($\frac{1}{2}$ inch) slices and lay them in a glass dish. Stir in the other ingredients, except the herbs, and leave to marinate in the fridge for at least an hour, stirring occasionally. Fifteen minutes before serving, drain and add the chopped herbs. Adjust the seasoning if necessary. Serve cool but not cold from the fridge.

corn bread

225g (8oz) cornmeal
225g (8oz) plain flour
2 tspns baking powder
1 tspn bicarbonate of soda
$\frac{1}{2}$ tspn salt
black pepper
1 large can sweetcorn (whizz half the quantity in a liquidizer)
142ml ($\frac{1}{4}$ pint) carton sour cream
2 eggs, beaten
125ml (4fl oz) milk
2 tbsp vegetable oil
1 rounded tbsp soft brown sugar
1 tbsp chopped jalapeño pepper

Set the oven to 180°C/375°F/gas mark 4. Butter and base-line a deep, 23cm (9in) diameter metal cake tin. Put all the dry ingredients, including the remainder of the sweetcorn, into a bowl. In another bowl mix the creamed corn with the sour cream, eggs, milk and oil. Pour the mix onto the dry ingredients and combine until smooth. Tip into the prepared tin and bake for about 25 minutes.

pan bagnat

This is traditionally made with crusty French bread, but for a change try it with ciabatta, focaccia or soda bread. Once wrapped tightly in cling film, it travels really well and provides a nourishing lunch bursting with flavour and texture. Prepare a few hours ahead or the night before.

1 wide French stick, or ciabatta loaves, or square or rectangular focaccia or soda bread loaves that give enough bread for 4–6 people
2–3 tablespoons good olive oil
1 clove garlic, crushed
2 orange peppers, grilled until blistered, and skinned
1 medium Spanish onion, very finely sliced into rings
225g (8oz) flavourful tomatoes, thinly sliced
1 x 275g (10oz) bottle marinated artichoke hearts, drained and sliced into 3 or 4 slices
a handful of black olives, stones removed and sliced
10–12 anchovy fillets
a large handful of fresh basil leaves, shredded
salt and freshly ground black pepper

Split the loaf or loaves into horizontal pieces, leaving the bread joined along one edge. Spread the olive oil and garlic over all surfaces of the bread. Layer the other ingredients evenly over the bread, scatter the basil leaves on top and season to taste with salt and pepper. Wrap tightly in cling film and place under a heavy weight in the fridge. When it is time to tuck in at the picnic, divide the loaf or loaves into equal portions with a sharp bread knife. Serve with a crisp green salad.

Pan bagnat is hearty picnic food that is made well in advance, avoiding a last-minute panic. A savoury tart, such as crème fraîche and herb (above), is always popular.

crème fraîche & herb tart

500g (1lb 2oz) packet of shortcrust pastry
350g (12oz) gruyere cheese
a handful each of parsley, tarragon, thyme, chives
3 large eggs
500ml (20fl oz) tub crème fraîche
1 large clove garlic
salt and pepper

Set the oven to 180°C/350°F/gas mark 4. Roll out the pastry and line a 23cm (9in) diameter metal quiche tin. Grate half the cheese finely and dice the other half. Chop the herbs finely. Beat the eggs and stir into the crème fraîche together with the grated cheese, crushed garlic, herbs, salt and pepper. Press the diced cheese into the base of the pastry and pour on the filling. Cook for approximately 40 minutes until puffed and golden brown.

peach, mango and raspberry fruit salad

Something fruity and summery is a must on a picnic. A raspberry tart fits the bill beautifully, as does a fresh fruit salad (above).

This fruit salad, with a passion-fruit dressing, is easy to prepare and the exotic fruits simply explode with flavour.

8 peaches, peeled, stoned and sliced
3 mangoes, peeled, stoned and cut into slivers
225g (8oz) fresh raspberries
for the dressing:
freshly squeezed juice of 3 sweet oranges
the pulp of 10 passion fruit
2 tbsp brandy
1–2 tbsp caster sugar (or more to taste)

Place the peach and mango slices and the raspberries into a lidded plastic box or bowl and wrap in cling film. Mix together the ingredients for the dressing in a separate box or screw-top jar and wrap in cling film or secure inside a plastic bag. When the picnickers are ready for dessert, simply pour the passion-fruit dressing over the fruit, stir carefully and serve.

mascarpone and raspberry tart

pastry:
400g (1lb) plain flour
50g (2oz) cornmeal
225g (8oz) unsalted butter
150g (6oz) icing sugar
1 egg
1 tbsp milk
filling:
400g (1lb) raspberries
2 large eggs
500g (1lb 2oz) mascarpone
1–2 tbsp vanilla sugar
1 dtspn flour

Whizz the flour, cornmeal and chopped butter in a food processor until the mixture resembles breadcrumbs. Add the sugar and combine again. Add the egg and milk and process until a ball is formed. Wrap in cling film and refrigerate for at least an hour. Roll out and line a 23cm (9in) metal tart tin. Line with baking beans and bake blind until light golden in colour. Strew the raspberries over the base. Beat together the eggs, mascarpone, sugar and flour and pour over the raspberries. Bake for 30–40 minutes until slightly browned and puffed.

inspired picnics

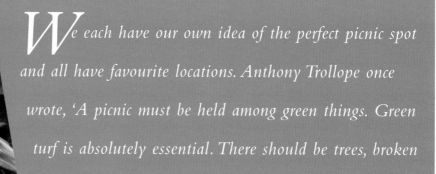

*W*e each have our own idea of the perfect picnic spot and all have favourite locations. Anthony Trollope once wrote, 'A picnic must be held among green things. Green turf is absolutely essential. There should be trees, broken

Dreamy and atmospheric, wonderful words to describe the inspired picnic. The Picnic, Little Dean was painted by Philip Wilson Steer (1860–1942), while the romantic image above appeared in an advertisement for rosé wine in 1973.

ground, small paths, thickets and hidden recesses. There should, if possible, be rocks, old timber, moss and brambles. There should certainly be hills and dales – on a small scale; and above all, there should be running water.' Charles Dickens described the perfect location as 'a green spot, on a big hill, carpeted with soft turf … shady trees, and heather and, as far as the eye could see, a rich landscape.'

Of course, not all picnics need soft turf, and different environments lend themselves to many different occasions.

The perfect setting for a feast beneath the stars is perhaps a softly landscaped garden or sweeping parkland; for a children's outing, open heathland or wooded countryside; and for barbecues and campfires, the beach or village green. And what could be better than lounging with friends on a rug in the corner of a hayfield, perched high on a craggy slope, or rocking gently in a boat. The important element is to be beneath the open sky, free to enjoy the scents and sounds, colours and textures, and the changing light of the setting.

evening alfresco

Romance could hardly fail to blossom in this delightful alfresco setting. Remember to take along a generous supply of anti-mosquito devices (above) to make sure the mood isn't ruined!

What could be more romantic than a deliciously indulgent candlelit picnic to accompany an open-air concert or an outdoor celebration on a summer evening? The secret to creating a fairyland ambience is to add to the picnic equipment a few lanterns, portable lamps, flares or candles. Picnickers can now decorate their picnic scene with neon drinking tumblers that light up at a shake, and glow sticks and spikes that hang from the branches of surrounding and overhanging trees or stand in tumblers and flowerpots. Conceal glowing fairy tea-lights inside coloured glass vases or frosted glass pillars that push into soil, grass or sand, and light anti-bug lanterns or citronella candles for the advantage they offer not only in casting a soft light but also in keeping mosquitoes away. Add a little forest magic with battery-powered humming birds and dragonflies that are mounted on an almost invisible spike and, once alight, appear to hover around you. Larger flares and naked candle flames need very careful handling but they add a dramatic flickering light to an alfresco entertainment in the evening. Remember to take a warm wrap so that, even when the air begins to cool, the enjoyment and romance of your candlelit evening is not lost.

cooking in the open air

The story-book children's picnic – a handsome boy in blazer and boater boils a kettle over a twig fire to make tea for his pretty, ladylike companions. The modern version (above), a colourful kebab cooked on a portable barbecue, is safer and more practical.

The ultimate in outdoor cooking is the good Girl Guide or Boy Scout's technique of choosing a safe place to light a fire, preparing the ground by carefully cutting and rolling back the turf, gathering armfuls of snap-dry kindling and larger twigs and branches, building a neat tepee of dry leaves and tiny twigs, and then coaxing the first flames to catch and grow into a fire that is compact and hot enough to bake potatoes tightly wrapped in foil, fry sausages and bacon, heat billycans of rice pudding and satisfy every hiker or rambler's hunger.

For those who prefer a little more comfort and luxury, portable stoves and small barbecues allow easy preparation of delicious hot picnic food. Single or double burner stoves, portable picnic grills and barbecues are available fuelled by gas, gel, diesel, wood or charcoal briquettes, so take your pick

and rustle up piping hot treats whenever and wherever you wish. And so that fingers don't get burned too often, easy-to-carry bags and boxes come ready packed with all the tongs, spatulas, slices, skewers, knives and forks that you might need for outdoor grilling. Remember to pack a burn spray or cream (just in case) and some practical means of carrying greasy implements home for washing.

'While Joe was slicing bacon for breakfast, Tom and Huck asked him to hold on a minute; they stepped to a promising nook in the riverbank and threw in their lines … They fried the fish with the bacon and were astonished; for no fish had ever seemed so delicious before ….'
Mark Twain,
The Adventures of Tom Sawyer,
1876

a picnic tea

Afternoon tea taken out of doors is one of the great pleasures of a summer's day. Fingers of home-made shortbread (above), served sprinkled with sugar and fresh lavender flowers, are the ideal accompaniment.

On a perfect summer's day, when the air is still and the countryside quietly listens to the music of birdsong and the murmur of bees, a delicious picnic tea completes the idyllic scene of peace and tranquillity. A little kettle on its spirit stove brings the water to a rolling boil, then the tea leaves in a pretty china pot release their colour and aroma to give a perfect brew that pairs refreshingly with egg-mayonnaise sandwiches, slices of fruit loaf spread with butter, crisp shortbread biscuits, baby macaroons and chocolate cake.

As the novelist Henry James wrote in 1881 in *The Portrait of a Lady*, 'Under certain circumstances, there are few hours in life more agreeable than the hour dedicated to the ceremony known as afternoon tea. There are circumstances in which – whether you partake of the tea or not – the situation is in itself delightful.' James recalls a picnic tea so pleasurable that the memory stayed with him for ever: 'The implements of the little feast had been disposed upon the lawn of an old English country house, in what I should call the perfect middle of a splendid summer afternoon.'

children's picnics

A tent is always exciting for children, conjuring up dreams of adventures with secret hiding places. Picnicware in bright colours (above) adds to the fun.

To entertain a bunch of lively children at a picnic, choose a location where there is plenty of room to run around and let off steam. Devise a menu that provides robust food that is filling and fun and present it in an unusual way – tiny sandwiches with colourful fillings on a kebab stick separated by baby tomatoes and cubes of cheese; crisps or kettle chips served inside a cornet of brightly coloured foil wrapping paper secured at the base with a little coloured plastic peg; or give each child a large platter that holds smaller cocktail dishes each filled with a different treat; or present each member of the group with his or her own individual picnic basket or box. Hand round cans or bottles of drink with brightly coloured curly plastic straws, and have plenty of kitchen towel, paper napkins and hand-wipes, ready to mop up any spills and wipe sticky fingers and mouths. For dessert, hide carefully wrapped sweets or little bags of treats among the surrounding trees and bushes and send the children off to hunt for their pudding – but always remember to have some spare for the less successful hunters.

'It was a very small bower – just big enough to hold them, and the baskets, and the kitten ... Katy untied and lifted the lid of the largest basket, while all the rest peeped eagerly to see what was inside.' (Inside they found ginger cake, buttered biscuits, cold lamb, hard-boiled eggs and bread and butter with corned beef.) 'Oh how good everything tasted in that bower ... Every mouthful was a pleasure.' Susan Coolidge, *What Katy Did* (published 1872)

a teddy-bears' picnic

We can really only guess what a teddy-bears' picnic might be like, but this human interpretation, featuring some very special and much-loved teddy bears, must surely come very close!

As everyone knows, a trip to the woods is bound to hold surprises and no one should venture down a forest path in summer unless they are clad in a very convincing teddy-bear disguise – for, according to Jimmy Kennedy's 1950s *Story of the Teddy Bears' Picnic*, 'way out in the woods' is where whole families of bears gather together for their annual picnic.

Apparently, the bears prepare for more than two months for their BIG EVENT in Cotton-tail's Wood – hunting for food, grinding the corn, growing the salads. The delectable menu always includes wild celery leaves mixed up with marshmallow flowers, sweet honeysuckle served with buttercup dressing, chocolate éclairs, platefuls of cherries, strawberries and cream, fruit, jams and jellies, and of course, lots of honey. And when they aren't actually getting very sticky paws

and noses, they play Chasing the Lion, Changing our Names, and Ring O' Roses, and they climb trees, hide in the bracken, dance and tumble and run races. What a wonderful picnic! And, of course, if any non-bears are frightened of what they might come across in the shadows of the woodland, it is all quite safe and quiet again after 6 o'clock because that's when all the Mummy and Daddy bears scoop up their sleepy offspring and whisk them off to be tucked into their beds.

Teddy-bears' picnics still happen today, of course, in and out of the woods, with events all over Britain during the summer months attended by excited children (including some quite grown-up ones) who bring their favourite bears and enjoy face painting, stilt walking, balloon modelling, 'guess the teddy's name' competitions and, of course, a yummy picnic.

literary picnics

A wonderful picnic by the riverside – an illustration by Peter Barrett from Kenneth Grahame's children's classic The Wind in the Willows. *A portly Mr Pickwick (above) enjoys a picnic in Dickens' Household Edition (1871–79) of* Pickwick Papers.

The timeless joy of the picnic is such that writers over the centuries have often created or recorded indulgent meals taken in the open air. Some tell of vast banquets at which copious quantities of food and drink have been consumed. Kenneth Grahame's Rat and Mole in *The Wind in the Willows* decide to spend the morning on the river. They take a 'fat wicker luncheon-basket' and Rat explains, 'There's cold chicken inside it … Andcoldtonguecold hamcoldbeefpickledgherkinssaladfrench rollscresssandwichespottedmeatginger beerlemonadesodawater-' to which Mole cries 'O stop, stop! This is too much!'

In *The Posthumous Papers of The Pickwick Club* (1837), Charles Dickens' Mr Weller enjoys 'Weal pie, wery good thing is weal pie when you know the lady as made it, and is quite sure it an't kittens … Tongue; well, that's a wery good thing when it an't a woman's …

Bread – knuckle o'ham, reg'lar picter – cold beef in slices, wery good.' Other literary picnics tell of more modest occasions. Poet John Taylor wrote in the 17th century: 'When Puddle-hill I footed downe, and past/A mile from thence, I found a hedge at last./There stroke we sayle our Bacon, Cheese and Bread,/We drew like Fidlers, and like farmers fed.' And Dorothy Wordsworth wrote in her Grasmere Journal in May 1802: 'We came down and rested upon a moss covered Rock, rising out of the bed of the River. There we lay, ate our dinner and stayed there till about 4 o'clock or later. Wm and C repeated and read verses. I drank a little Brandy and water and was in Heaven.'

Whatever the setting and ingredients, picnics in literature always convey the enhanced flavour of the food, the sense of freedom, and the simple pleasures of eating under the open sky.

useful addresses

R K ALLISTON
173 New Kings Road
London SW6 4SW
Tel 0207 731 8100
6 Quiet Street,
Bath, Somerset BA1 2JS
Tel 01225 421001
www.rkalliston.com
Stylish garden accessories
including lighting and
wasp traps

AMBERLEY BASKETS
Tel 01252 793389
www.amberleybaskets.co.uk
A really excellent range of
traditional picnic hampers,
priced from around £75 for a
basic model to over £500 for
an English willow hamper
fitted with bone china, crystal
glasses and useful accessories

THE DINING ROOM SHOP
63–64 White Hart Lane, Barnes
London SW13 OPZ
Tel 0208 878 1020
www.thediningroomshop.co.uk
A wonderful selection of
elegant china, glass, cutlery
and accessories

FORTNUM & MASON
181 Piccadilly, London W1A 1ER
Tel 0207 734 8040
www.fortnumandmason.com
Luxury food hampers with the
distinctive Fortnum & Mason
stamp, ranging in price from
below £75 to over £500 for
a truly indulgent, special-
occasion picnic

LAKELAND LTD
Alexandra Buildings
Windermere
Cumbria LA23 1BQ
Tel 015394 88100
www.lakelandlimited.com
Practical storage for spill-proof
picnics, as well as accessories
such as mesh food covers and
tablecloth clips

JOHN LEWIS/WAITROSE
Stores countrywide – locations
available on the following websites:
www.johnlewis.com
www.waitrose.com
Fun and functional picnicware,
garden furniture and accessories
available from John Lewis, and a
great range of picnic food and
drinks from Waitrose

THE NATIONAL TRUST

An excellent range of picnic accessories including backpacks (see p44), wine-coolers, flasks and waterproof rugs. Available at selected properties and high-street shops or by mail order from The National Trust shop at
41 High Street, Salisbury
Wilts SP1 2PB
Tel 01722 331884
www.nationaltrust.org.uk

LE MANOIR AUX QUAT'SAISONS

Church Road, Great Milton,
Oxfordshire OX44 7PD
Tel 01844 278881
www.manoir.com
Gourmet picnics for two from this famous restaurant to enhance a special day out in the Cotswolds

THE OPEN ROAD

Tel 0845 070 5142
www.theopenroad.co.uk
Classic car hire for a memorable outing in the countryside around Stratford-upon-Avon, and you can order a picnic packed in a wicker hamper from the company when you book

UNWINED

Tel 01949 844324
www.unwined-online.co.uk
An indulgent mail-order picnic created for you, or top-quality ingredients to help you create your own

acknowledgements

The publishers would like to thank the following:
Pippin Britz, for her creative cooking and styling and for supplying the recipes on pages 56, 58, 60 (below) and 62 (below); Caroline Arber for her wonderful photography; Sally Powell for her thoughtful art direction; R.K. Alliston and The Dining Room Shop (see page 78) for their generous loan of props.

Photographs are reproduced by kind permission of the following:
The Advertising Archive: pp6, 11, 30, 55, 64; Bridgeman Art Library: pp7 (Lords Gallery, London), 14 (Yale Center for British Art), 15 (Private Collection), 16 (Private Collection), 17 (Private Collection), 18 (National Library of Australia, Canberra), 21 (The Fine Art Society, London), 25 (Private Collection), 26 (Private Collection), 27 (Private Collection), 28 (Private Collection), 29 (British Museum, London), 31 (Bibliotheque Nationale, Paris), 33 (Private Collection), 35 (Private Collection), 36 (V&A Museum, London), 37 (V&A Museum, London), 38 (Private Collection), 39 (Mallett & Son Antiques Ltd), 41 (Private Collection), 42 (Stapleton Collection), 43 (Private Collection), 45 (Private Collection), 52 (Private Collection), 65 (Private Collection), 77 (Private Collection); Mark Buckingham: page motif throughout; John Crook: p34; Mary Evans Picture Library: pp 8, 12, 20, 22, 23, 24, 32, 69, 76; Fortnum & Mason: p53; Glasgow Museums (The Burrell Collection): p13; Jarrold Publishing (by Caroline Arber): front cover, pp 1, 3, 9, 10, 19, 40, 44, 46, 47, 48, 49, 51, 56, 57, 58, 59, 60, 61, 62, 63, 66, 67, 68, 70, 72, 73, 74, 75, endpapers; Period Living & Traditional Homes/Emap Consumer Media: 50, 54, 71, back cover.

Quotations are reproduced by kind permission of the following:
Palgrave Macmillan (page 8); The Random House Group Ltd (page 46, edited by William Plomer, published by Jonahan Cape).